Busy Ant Maths

2nd EDITION

Activity Book 1C

Date: _____

Name game

Read and write numbers from 1 to 20 in numerals and words

thirteen

seventeen

eleven

nineteen

fourteen

sixteen

twelve

eighteen

fifteen

twenty

Teacher's notes

Children read each number written on the t-shirts and write the same number in numerals into the space.

2

Date: _____

Plaice value

Recognise place value in numbers

You will need:
- coloured pencils

Teacher's notes

Children colour one portion of fish and one portion of chips to match the shirt of the customer buying them.

3

Counting more than 20

Count groups of more than 20 objects

Date: _____

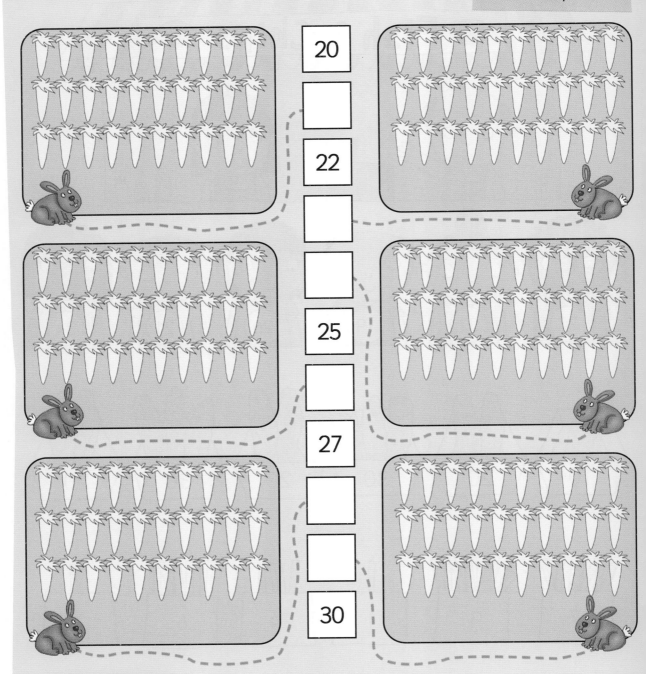

20
22
25
27
30

Teacher's notes

Children complete the number track from 20 to 30, writing the missing numbers into the spaces. Then they follow each rabbit's track, to find out how many carrots they need to count and colour in that field.

Counting machines

Count on or back in 2s, 5s and 10s

Date: _____

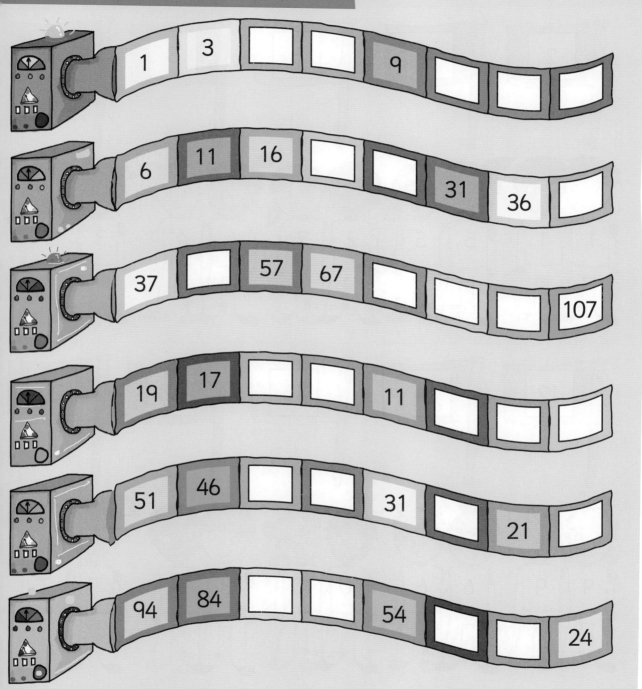

| 1 | 3 | | | 9 | | | |

| 6 | 11 | 16 | | | 31 | 36 | |

| 37 | | 57 | 67 | | | | 107 |

| 19 | 17 | | | 11 | | | |

| 51 | 46 | | | 31 | | 21 | |

| 94 | 84 | | | 54 | | | 24 |

Teacher's notes

Children complete the sequence for each counting machine by counting on or back in 2s, 5s or 10s.
Then they write the missing numbers in the spaces provided.

At the double!

Recall doubles of all numbers from 1 to 10

Date: _____

You will need:
• coloured pencils

In each section, children look at the numbers on each pair of runners' tops and work out the addition double. Then they find the finishing flag showing the answer to each pair and colour both tops to match.

Date: _____

Longship addition

Use doubles to help solve addition problems

7 + 8 =

4 + 5 =

6 + 7 =

5 + 6 =

8 + 9 =

6 + 6

8 + 8

7 + 7

4 + 4

5 + 5

Teacher's notes

Children solve the addition calculation on each Viking longship, using an addition double to help them. Then they continue the line from each ship to show the route to the addition double island that helped to solve the problem.

Any order

Date: _____

Understand that addition can be done in any order

0 1 2 3 4 5 6 7 8 9 10 11 12 13 14 15 16 17 18 19 20

☐ + ☐ + ☐ = 15

☐ + ☐ + ☐ = 17

☐ + ☐ + ☐ = 15

☐ + ☐ + ☐ = 17

☐ + ☐ + ☐ = 16

☐ + ☐ + ☐ = 18

☐ + ☐ + ☐ = 16

☐ + ☐ + ☐ = 18

Teacher's notes

For each question, children write three numbers which, when added together, make 15, 16, 17 or 18. They can use the penguin number track to help them.

8

Talented trios

Date: _____

Recall addition and subtraction facts to 20 and use them to work out other facts

You will need:
- paper

9   17   8

☐ + ☐ = ☐

☐ − ☐ = ☐

18   5   13

☐ + ☐ = ☐

☐ − ☐ = ☐

19   8   11

☐ + ☐ = ☐

☐ − ☐ = ☐

14   6   20

☐ + ☐ = ☐

☐ − ☐ = ☐

Teacher's notes

Children look at the numbers on each musical trio and write one addition and one subtraction fact using the three numbers. If appropriate, they then find the other two facts for each trio, writing the answers on a sheet of paper.

Date: _____

Where is Toby?

Use position words

Toby is...

[   ] the box.

[   ] the tree.

[   ] the hill.

[   ] the tent.

[   ] the wall.

[   ] the clock.

| on top of | underneath | in front of | behind | inside | outside |

Teacher's notes

Children look at each picture to decide where Toby is. Then they use the words and phrases at the bottom of the page to complete the sentences.

10

Date: _____

Where on the farm?

nderstand position words

You will need:
• coloured pencils

Draw:

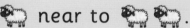 near to .

 far from .

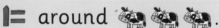 around  .

 close to  .

 and   far

 and   near

 and   around

Teacher's notes

Children follow the instructions to draw animals and objects in correct positions on the farm. Then they identify pairs of objects on the farm and draw a line to the best position word for each pair.

11

Hungry insects

Understand and use direction words

Date: _____

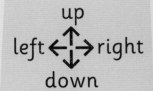

up
left ←→ right
down

	right →		down ↓

Teacher's notes

In the top section, children follow the directions for each insect from one leaf to another. Then they draw a line to match each insect to the fruit it eats. In the bottom section, children draw a circle around the one uneaten fruit from the first exercise. Then they use two words and/or two arrows to write instructions for each insect to reach the uneaten fruit.

12

Date: _____

View from a hill

Recognise and make whole, half, quarter and three-quarter turns

You will need:
• coloured pencils

sees ⊙ ⊙	turns	sees ⊙ ⊙
	quarter	
	three-quarter	
	half	

Teacher's notes

Children draw what the person on the hill will see when they make a turn to the right (clockwise), or write how far the person on the hill needs to turn to the right (clockwise) to see the second feature.

13

Kangaroo 2s

Count in steps of 2

Date: _____

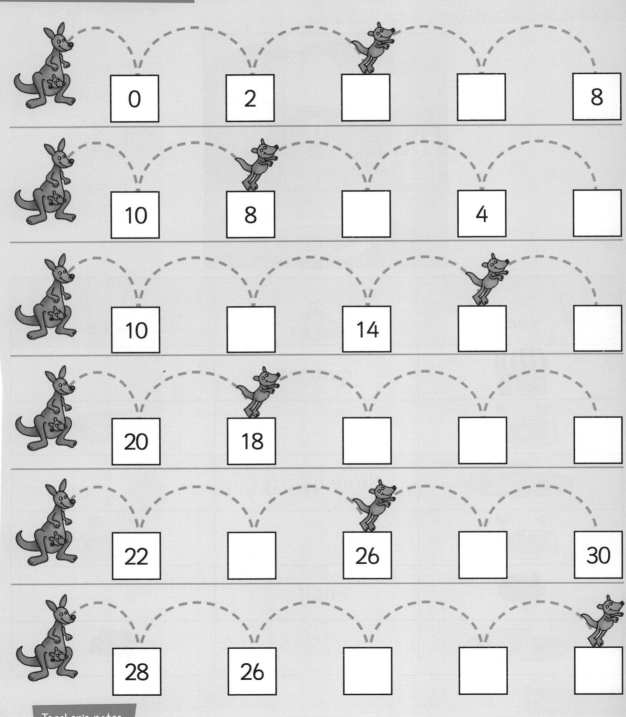

Row 1: 0 | 2 | ☐ | ☐ | 8

Row 2: 10 | 8 | ☐ | 4 | ☐

Row 3: 10 | ☐ | 14 | ☐ | ☐

Row 4: 20 | 18 | ☐ | ☐ | ☐

Row 5: 22 | ☐ | 26 | ☐ | 30

Row 6: 28 | 26 | ☐ | ☐ | ☐

Date: _____

Count groups of 2

Make connections between arrays,
number patterns and counting in 2s

You will need:
• coloured pencils

4 lots of 2

equals [ ] altogether.

9 lots of 2

equals [ ] altogether.

5 lots of 2

equals [ ] altogether.

8 lots of 2

equals [ ] altogether.

6 lots of 2

equals [ ] altogether.

10 lots of 2

equals [ ] altogether.

Teacher's notes

Children follow the instructions to draw and colour an array of counters in each grid.
They write the total number of counters in each array in the space provided.

15

Quilt counting

Count in steps of 5 and 10

Date: _____

Teacher's notes

In each row of the patchwork quilt, children count on or back in 5s or 10s and write the missing numbers in the spaces.

Date: _____

Apple arrays

Make connections between arrays, number patterns and counting in 5s and 10s

You will need:
- red or green coloured pencils

Show an array of 10.

Show an array of 15.

Show an array of 30.

Show an array of 20.

Show an array of 25.

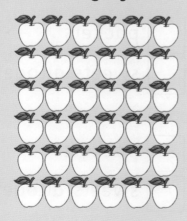

Show an array of 35.

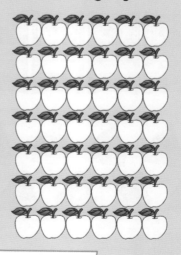

Teacher's notes

Children colour the apples in red or green to show the arrays in each section.

17

Sweet shop groups

Date: _____

Find a total by counting groups of 2, 5 or 10

2 sweets

5 sweets

10 sweets

☐ packets
☐ sweets altogether

☐ packets
☐ sweets altogether

☐ packets
☐ sweets altogether

☐ packets
☐ sweets altogether

☐ packets
☐ sweets altogether

Teacher's notes

For each group of sweets, children count and write down how many packets there are. Then they count in 2s, 5s or 10s to find out how many sweets there are altogether in each group.

18

Date: _____

Solving shopping problems

Count groups of 2, 5 or 10 to solve problems

There are 2 socks in each pair. There are 8 pairs.

There are ☐ socks altogether.

There are 5 pens in each pot. There are 6 pots.

There are ☐ pens altogether.

There are 10 sweets in 1 bag. There are 7 bags.

There are ☐ sweets altogether.

Sam has collected 2p coins. He has 9 coins.

Sam has ☐ p altogether.

Halle has 5 books on each shelf. She has 7 shelves.

Halle has ☐ books altogether.

Ellis has 10 stickers on each page. There are 9 pages altogether.

Ellis has ☐ stickers altogether.

Teacher's notes

Children read each problem and complete them by counting in groups of 2, 5 or 10.

Cookie shares

Share objects into equal groups

Date: _____

| shared between | is | . | shared between | is | |

| shared between | is | . | shared between | is | |

Teacher's notes

Children count the number of cookies in the group, then share them equally between the trays by drawing them onto each one. Then, they complete the sentence underneath.

Fair shares

Date: _____

Solve problems involving equal sharing

Toffee apples

☐ toffee apples shared between ☐ makes ☐ each.

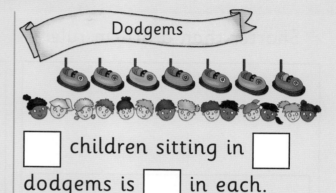

Dodgems

☐ children sitting in dodgems is ☐ in each.

Helter skelter

Ella buys 14 tickets.
She shares them between 7.

☐ shared between ☐ is ☐.

Cups and saucers

☐ children sitting in cups and saucers is ☐ in each cup.

Candy floss

☐ candy flosses shared between ☐ makes ☐ each.

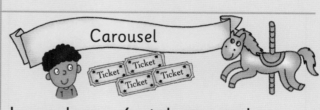

Carousel

Leon buys 4 tickets and spends 20p. ☐p shared between ☐ is ☐p.

Teacher's notes

Children read each problem involving equal sharing and solve it by writing the correct numbers and answers in the boxes underneath.

The ruler and the metre rule

Date: _____

Measure using a ruler and understand what a metre rule is

You will need:
- ruler
- metre rule

Shorter than a 30 cm ruler

Longer than a 30 cm ruler

Shorter than a metre

Longer or taller than a metre

Teacher's notes

At the top of the page children draw pictures of two objects that are shorter and two objects that are longer than a 30 centimetre ruler. Then they measure the real objects and write the lengths underneath their drawings. At the bottom of the page children draw pictures of objects that are shorter and longer or taller than a metre rule.

Estimating and measuring

Estimate and measure lengths and heights

Date: _____

You will need:
- ruler
- metre rule
- glue stick
- book
- scissors
- small bottle
- chair

Object	Estimate	Measurement
glue stick		
book		
scissors		
bottle		

chair

Teacher's notes

Children estimate the length or height of each real object. Then they use a 30 centimetre ruler to measure the actual length/height. They write their estimates and measurements in the appropriate spaces in the table. Then children use a metre rule to measure the height of a chair.

23

How many bricks?

Date: _____

Solve problems about mass

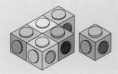

2 blocks

5 blocks

1 block

3 blocks

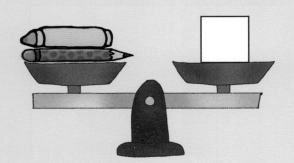
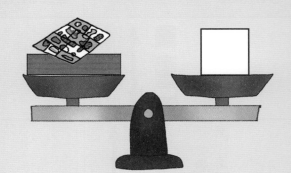

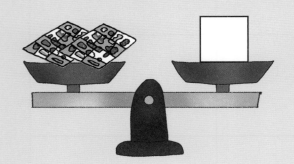
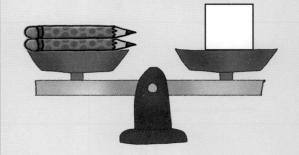

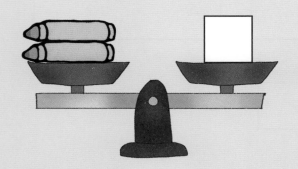
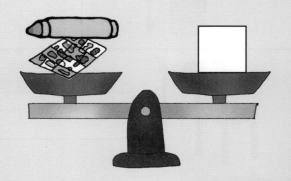

24

Date: _____

Shapes that balance

Solve problems about mass

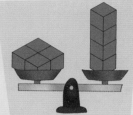

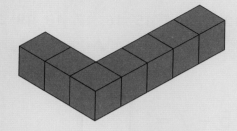

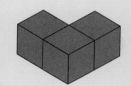

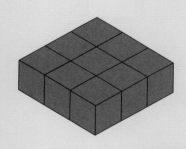

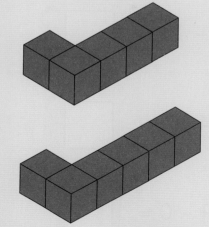

Teacher's notes

Children draw lines to show shapes that would balance on a pan balance.

25

Monkey mix-up

Recall addition and subtraction facts to 20

0 1 2 3 4 5 6 7 8 9 10 11 12 13 14 15 16 17 18 19 20

11 + 3 = ☐

15 − 7 = ☐

12 − 2 = ☐

9 + 8 = ☐

14 + 1 = ☐

18 − 9 = ☐

13 − 0 = ☐

11 + 5 = ☐

12 + 4 = ☐

20 − 13 = ☐

14 − 3 = ☐

7 + 11 = ☐

16 + 4 = ☐

19 − 0 = ☐

Teacher's notes

Children work out the answer to each addition or subtraction calculation, writing their answer in the box.
If necessary, they use the 0–20 number track to support their thinking.

rain patterns

Date: _____

ecognise patterns in addition and subtraction

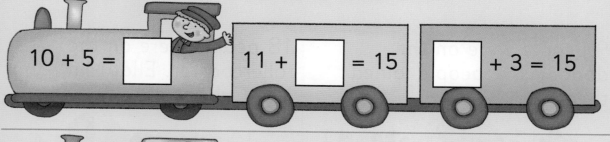

10 + 5 = ☐   11 + ☐ = 15   ☐ + 3 = 15

16 − 6 = ☐   16 − ☐ = 9   16 − 8 = ☐

9 + 8 = ☐   10 + ☐ = 17   11 + ☐ = 17

19 − 7 = ☐   19 − 8 = ☐   19 − ☐ = 10

17 + 3 = ☐   16 + ☐ = 20   ☐ + 5 = 20

Teacher's notes

Children complete the addition or subtraction pattern shown on each set of engine and carriages, writing the correct numbers in the boxes.

Fairground problems

Solve word problems

Date: _____

9 people were on the dodgems. 7 people joined them.

How many people were on the dodgems altogether?

18 people were on the rollercoaster. Ella, Min, Amir and Cal got off.

How many people were left on the rollercoaster?

There were 20 toffee apples. Emma bought 2 of them.

How many toffee apples were left?

There were 12 prizes on the top shelf and 8 more on the bottom shelf.

How many prizes were there altogether?

Teacher's notes

Children read each word problem. Then they write the addition or subtraction calculation in the boxes.

Date: _____

Add and takeaway menu

Solve problems involving money

Menu

 10p

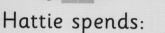 8p

 11p

 9p

 12p

 7p

 4p

Hattie spends:

☐ ◯ ☐ ◯ ☐

Her change is:

☐ ◯ ☐ ◯ ☐

Yuko spends:

☐ ◯ ☐ ◯ ☐

Her change is:

☐ ◯ ☐ ◯ ☐

Caie spends:

☐ ◯ ☐ ◯ ☐

His change is:

☐ ◯ ☐ ◯ ☐

Cavan spends:

☐ ◯ ☐ ◯ ☐

His change is:

☐ ◯ ☐ ◯ ☐

Teacher's notes

Children look at the menu. Each child has 20p to spend. They first work out how much each child spends and then calculate the change they each receive.

29

Yoyo spending

Date: _____

Recall addition and subtraction facts to 20

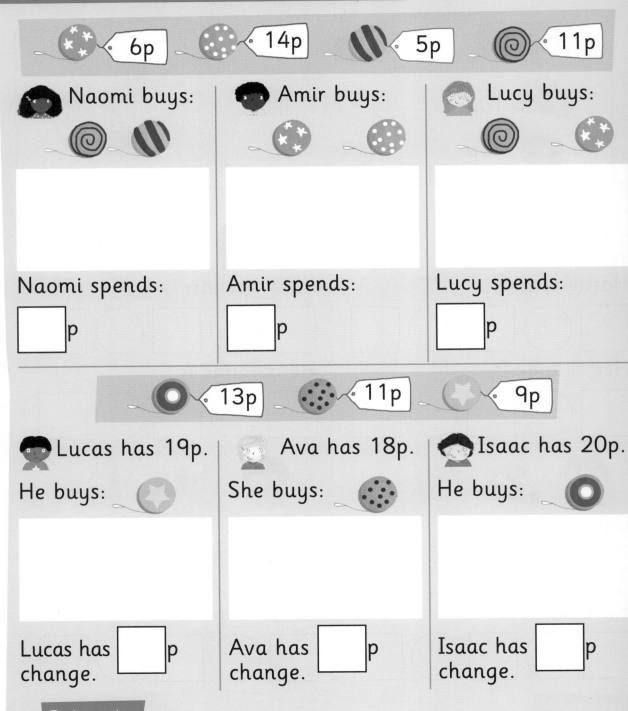

6p   14p   5p   11p

Naomi buys:

Amir buys:

Lucy buys:

Naomi spends:

☐ p

Amir spends:

☐ p

Lucy spends:

☐ p

13p   11p   9p

Lucas has 19p.

He buys:

Ava has 18p.

She buys:

Isaac has 20p.

He buys:

Lucas has ☐ p change.

Ava has ☐ p change.

Isaac has ☐ p change.

Teacher's notes

Children look at each addition or subtraction problem in turn and use the space underneath to work out each one, writing the answer in the box.

30

Date: _____

enny Lane

olve problems involving money

5p 10p 7p 2p 3p 4p 6p 11p

Thea had 18p.
Her change was 8p.

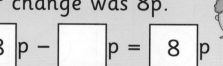

| 18 |p − | | |p = | 8 |p |

Thea bought:

Ethan bought 2 items.
He spent 14p.

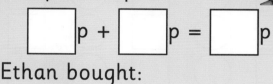

| | |p + | | |p = | | |p |

Ethan bought:

Max had 20p.
His change was 15p.

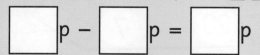

| | |p − | | |p = | | |p |

Max bought:

Ruby bought 2 items.
She spent 17p.

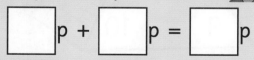

| | |p + | | |p = | | |p |

Ruby bought:

Teacher's notes

Children complete the addition or subtraction problem to find out which item or items each character buys. They draw the item or items into the space underneath each one.

Pyramid puzzles

Date: _____

Recall related addition and subtraction facts

8 17 9

6 12 18

19 9 10

13 20 7

Teacher's notes

Children use the numbers on each pyramid to write four related facts – two addition facts and two subtraction facts.

dd on l0, take off l0

dd and subtract 10 to or from a number

Date: _____

You will need:
- coloured pencils

1	2	3	4	5	6	7	8	9	10
11	12	13	14	15	16	17	18	19	20
21	22	23	24	25	26	27	28	29	30
31	32	33	34	35	36	37	38	39	40
41	42	43	44	45	46	47	48	49	50

3 + 10 = ☐

☐ + 10 = ☐

☐ + 10 = ☐

☐ + 10 = ☐

☐ + 10 = ☐

18 − 10 = ◯

◯ − 10 = ◯

◯ − 10 = ◯

◯ − 10 = ◯

◯ − 10 = ◯

Teacher's notes

Referring to the 1–50 grid, children find each number with a square around it, and add 10 to the number, drawing a square around the answer in the same colour. Then they complete each calculation as an addition fact in the boxes. Next, they look at each number that has been circled on the grid, and subtract 10 from the number, drawing a circle around the answer in the same colour. Finally, they complete each calculation as a subtraction fact.

33

2-D shape patterns

Complete 2-D shape patterns

Date: _____

You will need:
- coloured pencils

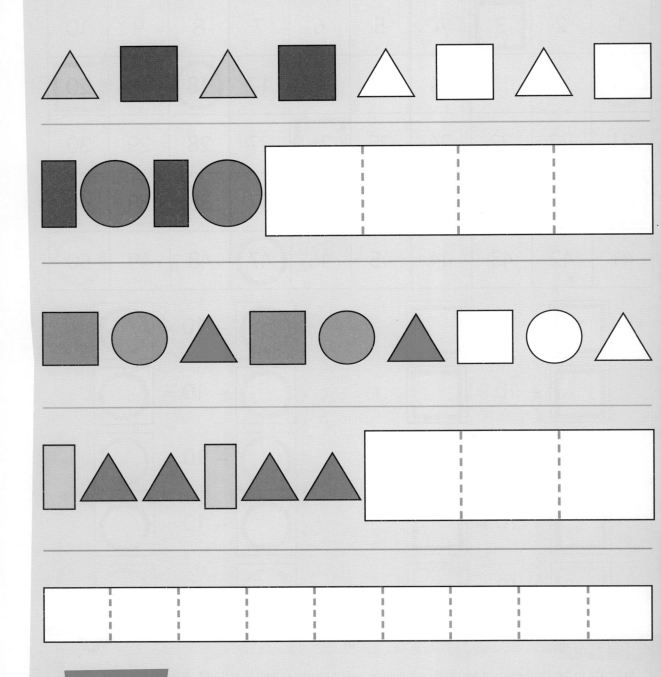

Teacher's notes

Children colour the shapes to continue the colour pattern or draw and colour the shapes within the boxes to complete a pattern. Finally, they make up their own shape and colour pattern.

Name that 2-D shape

Name 2-D shapes

Date: _____

| rectangle | circle | triangle | square |

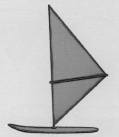

3-D shape patterns and models

Make patterns and models using 3-D shapes

Date: _____

You will need:
- coloured pencils
- 3-D shapes: cuboids, cubes, pyramids, spheres, cylinders and cones
- camera

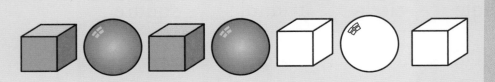

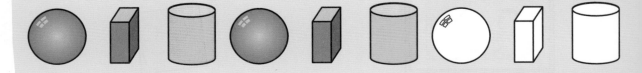

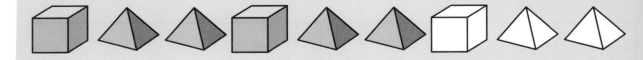

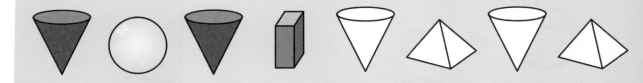

Date: _____

Name that 3-D shape

Name 3-D shapes

cone　　　cylinder　　　sphere
pyramid　　　cuboid　　　cube

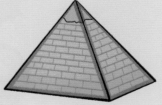

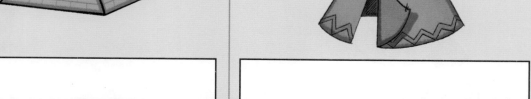

Pirate hat doubles

Double numbers to 10

Date: _____

Teacher's notes

Children draw a line to match each pirate to the parrot that shows double the number on their hat.

Pirate halves

Find half of a number or group of objects

Date: _____

Half of 8 is ⬜ .

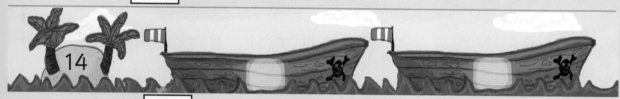

Half of 14 is ⬜ .

Half of 12 is ⬜ .

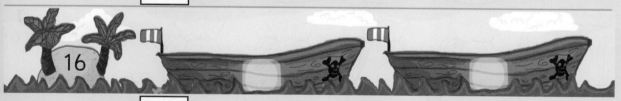

Half of 16 is ⬜ .

Half of 20 is ⬜ .

 Teacher's notes

Children look at the number on each island, which represents the number of pirates that need to go in the boats. Then they draw half the pirates in one boat and half in the other. Then they complete the sentence to find half of each number.

Date: _____

Treasure troves

Find one quarter of a number or group of objects

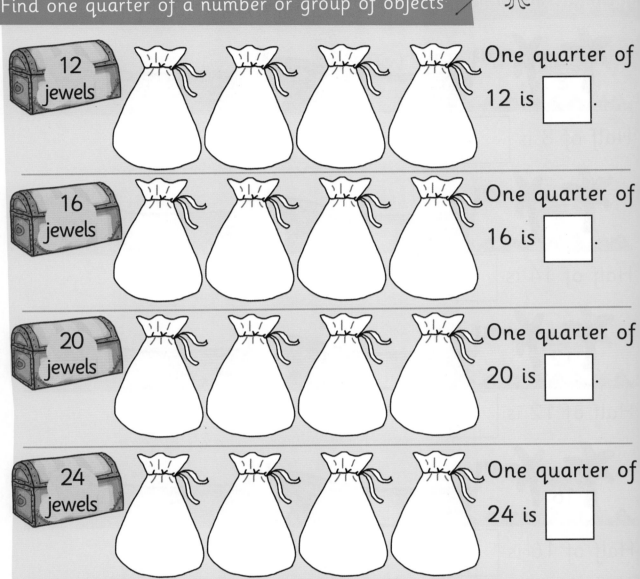

12 jewels — One quarter of 12 is ▢.

16 jewels — One quarter of 16 is ▢.

20 jewels — One quarter of 20 is ▢.

24 jewels — One quarter of 24 is ▢.

28 jewels — One quarter of 28 is ▢.

Teacher's notes

Children look at the number of jewels in each treasure chest, and then share them equally between the fo[ur] bags by drawing them in the spaces, to find one quarter. Then they complete each sentence to show one quarter of each group of jewels.

Doubles, halves and quarters

Date: _____

Find doubles, halves and quarters of numbers

Caie buys 2 fish stickers. Each one cost 7p. How much does he spend?

Ayesha has 8 charms on her bracelet – half of her charm collection. How many charms does she have altogether?

Laura has 12 sweets – double the number of sweets Amber has. How many does Amber have?

Cavan shares 16 biscuits into quarters. How many biscuits does he give to each friend?

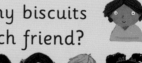

Patrick has 20 cars. He gives half of his collection to Lee. How many does he give to Lee?

Ciara has 20 stickers. She gives one quarter of them to Isaac. How many stickers does she give to Isaac?

Teacher's notes

Children read each problem carefully and decide whether it is a double, halve or quarter problem. Then they work out the answer, using the space underneath each problem to show their working out.

Cake quarters and halves

Find one half and one quarter of a shape

You will need:
- ruler
- coloured pencils

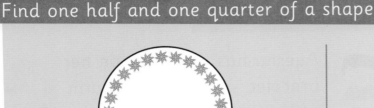

Divide the cake in half.
Colour one half.

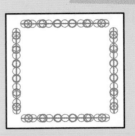

Divide the cake into quarters.
Colour one quarter.

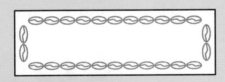

Divide the cake in half.
Colour one half.

Divide the cake into quarters.
Colour one quarter.

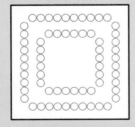

Divide the cake into quarters.
Colour three quarters.

Divide the cake into quarters.
Colour half of the cake.

Teacher's notes

Children follow the instructions to divide each cake into halves or quarters, drawing lines to divide each one. Then they colour the fraction of the cake specified.

Date: _____

Halves and quarters questions

Find one half and one quarter of a group of objects

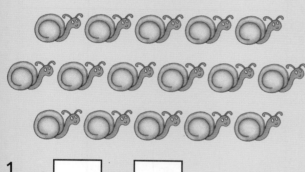

$\frac{1}{2}$ of ☐ is ☐ .

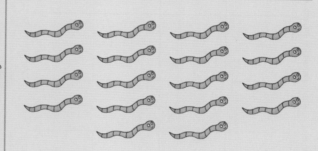

$\frac{1}{4}$ of ☐ is ☐ .

$\frac{1}{4}$ of ☐ is ☐ .

$\frac{1}{2}$ of ☐ is ☐ .

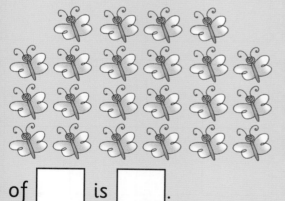

$\frac{1}{2}$ of ☐ is ☐ .

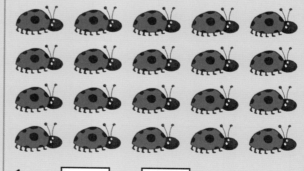

$\frac{1}{4}$ of ☐ is ☐ .

43

Flying carpet fractions

Recognise halves and quarters

Date: _____

You will need:
- coloured pencil

Date: _____

Party fractions

Understand that fractions are related to grouping and sharing

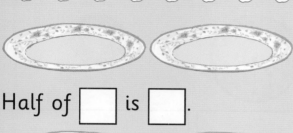

Half of ☐ is ☐.

One quarter of ☐ is ☐.

Half of ☐ is ☐.

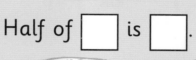

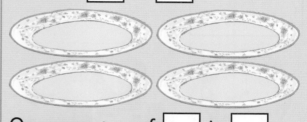

One quarter of ☐ is ☐.

$\frac{1}{2}$ of ☐ is ☐.

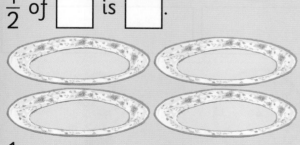

$\frac{1}{4}$ of ☐ is ☐.

$\frac{1}{2}$ of ☐ is ☐.

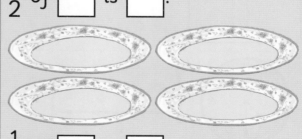

$\frac{1}{4}$ of ☐ is ☐.

Teacher's notes

Children count the total number of each item of party food. Then they share this number equally between the two plates by drawing them onto the plates to find half, and then complete each sentence underneath. Next, they share the total number equally between four plates by drawing them onto the plates to find one quarter of each, completing each sentence underneath.

45

What time is it?

Date: _____

Read times on clocks and understand time intervals

$\frac{1}{2}$ hour later	$\frac{1}{2}$ hour earlier	1 hour later	1 hour earlier

Teacher's notes

Children look at each clock and write the time. Then they choose one of the vocabulary labels to write in the final box to describe the time interval between the two events shown.

Date: _____

Drawing hands

Read and draw hands on clocks to show the time to the hour and half hour

 ← 1 hour earlier  1 hour later →

 ← 1 hour earlier  1 hour later →

 ← 1 hour earlier  1 hour later →

 ← 1 hour earlier  1 hour later →

 ← 1 hour earlier  1 hour later →

Teacher's notes

Children draw times on the clock faces to show the earlier or later times as shown on the arrows.

47

Date: _____

What can I do in 1 minute and 1 hour?

Begin to understand how long 1 minute and 1 hour are

minute

hour

About 1 minute	About 1 hour

Teacher's notes

Children look at each picture then draw a line to show whether the activity would last about 1 minute or 1 hour. Then they draw something else that lasts about 1 minute and about 1 hour.

Journey times

Solve problems relating to time

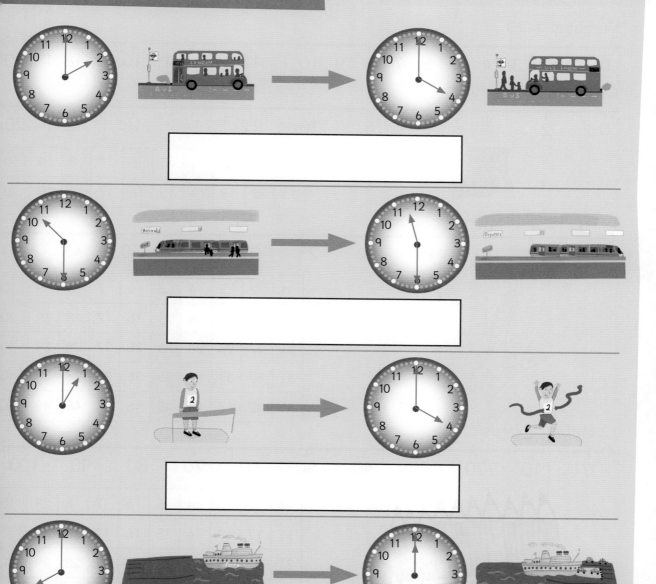

For each question, children look at the times shown on each clock and work out the difference in time between each journey. They write their answer in the box provided, e.g. 2 hours.

Maths facts

Numbers 0–20

0 1 2 3 4 5 6 7 8 9 10 11 12 13 14 15 16 17 18 19 20

Counting in steps of 2

0 2 4 6 8 10 12 14 16 18 20

1	2	3	4	5	6	7	8	9	10
11	12	13	14	15	16	17	18	19	20

Counting in steps of 5

0 5 10 15 20 25 30 35 40 45 50

1	2	3	4	5	6	7	8	9	10
11	12	13	14	15	16	17	18	19	20
21	22	23	24	25	26	27	28	29	30
31	32	33	34	35	36	37	38	39	40
41	42	43	44	45	46	47	48	49	50

Counting in steps of 10

0 10 20 30 40 50 60 70 80 90 100

1	2	3	4	5	6	7	8	9	10
11	12	13	14	15	16	17	18	19	20
21	22	23	24	25	26	27	28	29	30
31	32	33	34	35	36	37	38	39	40
41	42	43	44	45	46	47	48	49	50
51	52	53	54	55	56	57	58	59	60
61	62	63	64	65	66	67	68	69	70
71	72	73	74	75	76	77	78	79	80
81	82	83	84	85	86	87	88	89	90
91	92	93	94	95	96	97	98	99	100

Addition and subtraction facts to 5, 10 and 20

+	0	1	2	3	4	5	6	7	8	9	10
0	0	1	2	3	4	5	6	7	8	9	10
1	1	2	3	4	5	6	7	8	9	10	11
2	2	3	4	5	6	7	8	9	10	11	12
3	3	4	5	6	7	8	9	10	11	12	13
4	4	5	6	7	8	9	10	11	12	13	14
5	5	6	7	8	9	10	11	12	13	14	15
6	6	7	8	9	10	11	12	13	14	15	16
7	7	8	9	10	11	12	13	14	15	16	17
8	8	9	10	11	12	13	14	15	16	17	18
9	9	10	11	12	13	14	15	16	17	18	19
10	10	11	12	13	14	15	16	17	18	19	20

+	11	12	13	14	15	16	17	18	19	20
0	11	12	13	14	15	16	17	18	19	20
1	12	13	14	15	16	17	18	19	20	
2	13	14	15	16	17	18	19	20		
3	14	15	16	17	18	19	20			
4	15	16	17	18	19	20				
5	16	17	18	19	20					
6	17	18	19	20						
7	18	19	20							
8	19	20								
9	20									

4 o'clock

$\frac{1}{2}$ past 8

Fractions

Half: $\frac{1}{2}$

8	

Quarter: $\frac{1}{4}$

12			

2-D shapes

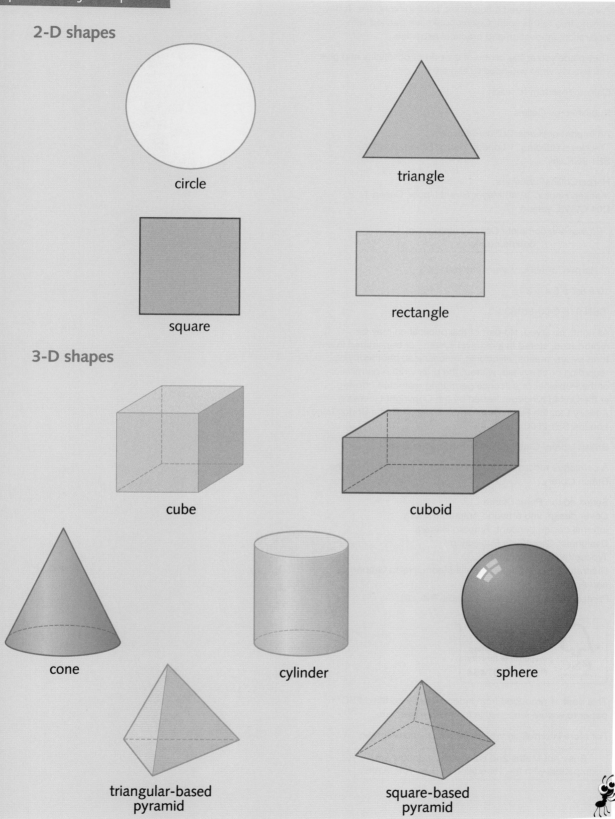

circle

triangle

square

rectangle

3-D shapes

cube

cuboid

cone

cylinder

sphere

triangular-based
pyramid

square-based
pyramid

William Collins' dream of knowledge for all began with the publication of his first book in 1819.

A self-educated mill worker, he not only enriched millions of lives, but also founded a flourishing publishing house. Today, staying true to this spirit, Collins books are packed with inspiration, innovation and practical expertise.

They place you at the centre of a world of possibility and give you exactly what you need to explore it.

Collins. Freedom to teach.

Published by Collins

An imprint of HarperCollins*Publishers*
The News Building, 1 London Bridge Street, London,
SE1 9GF, UK

HarperCollins*Publishers*
Macken House, 39/40 Mayor Street Upper, Dublin 1,
D01 C9W8, Ireland

Browse the complete Collins catalogue at
collins.co.uk

10 9 8 7 6 5 4 3 2

ISBN 978-0-00-861330-3

British Library Cataloguing-in-Publication Data

A catalogue record for this publication is available from the British Library.

Series editor: Peter Clarke
Cover design and artwork: Amparo Barrera
Internal design concept: Amparo Barrera
Designers: GreenGate Publishing
Typesetter: David Jimenez
Illustrators: Helen Poole, Natalia Moore, Helen Graper and Aptara
Printed in India by Multivista Global Pvt. Ltd.

MIX
Paper | Supporting responsible forestry
FSC™ C007454
www.fsc.org

This book is produced from independently certified FSC™ paper to ensure responsible forest management.

For more information visit: harpercollins.co.uk/green

Busy Ant Maths 2nd edition components are compatible with the 1st edition of Busy Ant Maths.